W.O.W.

Women of Worth Anthology

Dr. Yvonne Henderson

W.O.W. Women of Worth

Anthology

Copyright © 2024 by Dr. Yvonne Henderson

All rights reserved. No part of this publication may be reproduced, distributed, or transmitted in any form or by any means, including photocopying, recording, or other electronic or mechanical methods, without the prior written permission of the publisher, except in the case of brief quotations embodied in critical reviews and certain other noncommercial uses permitted by copyright laws. Unless otherwise indicated, scripture references are from the King James Bible Version.

Transitions Publishing

Missouri City TX 77459

Table of Contents

Dedication	**Page 4**
Introduction	**Page 5**
Worth (Dr. Yvonne Henderson)	**Page 7**
Through It All (Salena Glenn)	**Page 13**
Life Is But A Dream (Tamela Funchess)	**Page 21**
The Irony of Life (Dr. Barbara Bracy)	**Page 33**
Driven and Free (Tanya J. Haynes)	**Page 37**
I Didn't Know It Was Me (Jessica Lockett)	**Page 50**
My Cross of Leadership (Erica Bennett)	**Page 55**
Failure Is Not Final (Dr. Yvonne Henderson)	**Page 77**

Dedication

To the resilient, the trailblazers, the quiet forces of strength, and the unsung heroes—this anthology is dedicated to the Women of Worth. In every corner of the world, in every sphere of life, your stories unfold as a testament to the indomitable spirit and boundless worth that defines you.

To the mothers who sow love, the daughters who dream, the sisters who stand, and the friends who uplift—your worth is immeasurable, and your contributions are the threads that weave the fabric of our shared humanity.

To the visionaries who break barriers, the innovators who defy limits, and the advocates who champion justice—your worth is the force that propels progress and inspires generations to come.

May these pages echo with the strength of your voices, the richness of your experiences, and the beauty of your worth. In celebrating you, we celebrate the resilience, power, and enduring legacy of Women of Worth everywhere.

With gratitude for the past, reverence for the present, and hope for the future, this anthology is dedicated to the remarkable women who shape our world and remind us all of the infinite worth inherent in every woman.

Dr. Yvonne Henderson

Introduction

In the tapestry of human existence, there exists an exquisite thread woven with strength, resilience, and grace – the essence of a Woman of Worth. As we embark on this remarkable journey through the pages of "Women of Worth: An Anthology of Women," we are invited to explore the multifaceted facets of a woman's worth, illuminated by the inspiring stories, voices, and experiences of women from across the spectrum of life.

A woman's worth transcends mere quantifiable measures; it is a radiant, enduring flame that burns brightly in the face of adversity, injustice, and inequality. It is a testament to the indomitable spirit, the unyielding determination, and the boundless love that women infuse into every corner of our world. This anthology is a celebration of their profound contributions, their triumphs, and their enduring legacies that have left an indelible mark on our collective history.

In the pages that follow, you will meet a tapestry of women who have shattered ceilings, defied expectations, and blazed trails that guide us toward a future of greater equity and understanding. Their stories will resonate with readers of all backgrounds, transcending boundaries of race, age, and gender, for the worth of a woman is not limited by labels but rather defined by the immeasurable impact she leaves on society. As we delve into the narratives within "Women of Worth," may we be inspired, challenged, and uplifted by the voices of these remarkable women. Their stories remind us that a woman's worth is not static; it evolves, adapts, and grows stronger with each challenge faced and each barrier surmounted. Their experiences illuminate the complex tapestry of identity, heritage, and demonstrates that there is no single mold for a Woman of Worth. She is, in fact, as diverse and multifaceted as the world itself.

So, dear reader, join us on this transformative journey through the pages of "Women of Worth," and let the stories within remind us of all that a woman's worth is immeasurable, undeniable, and forever woven into the fabric of our shared human experience.

You may resonate with one story over another, but there is something for every woman to take hold of and identify with. The struggles being told are not unique but transcending. You may be going through something similar, or you may have gone through something similar, the beauty of it all is that we overcome by the telling of our testimony. Our struggles are not just for us, but for those around us, who need to know this is not the end, there is victory after this. Remember, although we may all come from different backgrounds, upbringings, or the other side of town, we can all relate to a woman's worth.

Worth

By Dr. Yvonne Henderson

What is worth? Worth is the value equivalent to that of someone or something under consideration, the level at which someone deserves to be valued or rated.?

What is value? As a noun it is a person's principles or standards of behavior; one's judgment of what is important in life. (They internalize their parents' rules as values.) What do you do when the parents you value are the ones who devalue you and strip you of your worth?

As a verb value allows you to consider (someone or something) to be important or `beneficial to your life.

What is your worth? What is the value of your life?

As women we tend to fall victim to people, especially men to validate our worth. We will indulge in abusive relationships be it physical or mental and not know how to get out because we feel we deserve it to some degree. Maybe it was something said or done in our childhood that made us feel a certain way. Someone touched you and you were told to keep quiet, this is our secret, no one else needs to know. You are special, that's why I'm doing this to you. If you say anything they won't believe you. You begin to believe the lies being told to you, so when you get older and try to have a relationship you don't think you are loved because they are not lying to you or putting their hands on you. You have become numb to who you are and are now being controlled by the actions of another. Something in you says run, but your body will not respond.

How did we get her? How do we get out?

- We must learn how to receive compliments. You may say that's easy, but it isn't. When you have been verbally abused and told over and over that you are worthless. No one will ever want you, that's why you are stuck with me You ugly! It takes a lot of strength to accept a compliment.
- Keep a journal, write down the things that you are and the things you are not, so yu can start coming into agreement with what you believe and dispel all the things you do not come to agreement with.
- Begin to affirm yourself. Tell yourself you are loved, you are powerful, you are great, you are more than what they say you are. You are above and not beneath. You are the head and not the tail. You are blessed in the city and blessed in the field Deuteronomy 28. I am fearfully and wonderfully made Psalm 139. These are the things that God believes about us. So, if He who created us feels

this way about us, why do we let an insignificant human tell us otherwise?

You may have an expertise in a certain field and find yourself taking a back seat to allow others shine even when the work done was yours. You are constantly performing at a high level with no recognition. You have provided training and programing for a company that you could run with your eyes closed. You have thoughts of starting your own business and you are told you aren't good enough. Have you ever stopped to ask yourself why others would say that when you are running their company. I'll tell you why they say it. They say it because they don't want the competition. They say it because they fear what you have the capability to do to their business if you start your own. You are a threat to them because you make them look good, just imagine what you would do for yourself if you left.

Don't think about it anymore, take back what belongs to you. Your worth, your value, start that business, step out on faith, and trust God to do what He said He will do. Get out of your own way and just do it. You will be surprised at what you can do. I know, I know it's new, you're scared. We all get scared, I would be lying if I said otherwise, but the difference is, God has not given us the spirit of fear, but of power, and love and of a sound mind 2 Timothy 1:7.

- You must believe in yourself. After hearing you were nothing for so long it may take you some time, but you can do it. Begin to write down what it is you want out of life, and how you see yourself accomplishing it. They say write your vision down so you can see it manifest, or you could create a vision board. Write positive thoughts or scriptures on sticky notes or paper and tape them around the house. Particularly in places that you frequent.

You may feel unworthy because you cannot have a child, or you've been told you can't have one. You're married and want a child; you try and try with no success. You begin to feel like less of a woman and wonder if he will stay. You do everything in your power to keep him happy and to make things worse, he cheats on you anyway. He plays with your mind and begins to abuse you mentally and emotionally. You feel worthless.

You may have been rapped; you don't say anything because you feel ashamed. You feel like it should not have happened to you. You know all the right things to do, yet it happens to you anyway, not once, but twice in your life. You feel tainted, belittled, and useless. Having an intimate relationship with a man is difficult because you don't want him to touch you, of if he does touch you, you feel dirty. You feel like you are not desirable. You feel like he doesn't respect you and does not value you or see your worth not only as a woman, but as a person. Your mind tells you that you are not desirable, and he sees you flawed. Your mind begins to play tricks on you and causes you to make decisions and choices that will not lead to a loving relationship. The self-talk you may have will tell you, you are not worthy of a loving caring relationship with a man. You see love in other places or in other ways, drinking, drugs, sexual escapades, or any other thing that p eases your fleshly desires. Unfortunately, none of it makes you feel better. You find yourself crying in the middle of the night seeking answers. You feel as though God has deserted you and you are alone. This is when God has your attention and can show you who He is and what He can do for you if you let Him. God can lift you from the muck and miry clay and He places your feet on a solid rock to stand. He can move mountains and obstacles out of your way. This is the time to surrender and say, Lord have Your way.

The stories you are about to read are true stories from real women who have walked through these things and discovered their worth in the process. So, Women of Worth, stand up and take your rightful place, it's time not only be seen, but to be heard.

God gave me a vision to empower women and I ran with it. This was my first anthology, and it has been a journey. A good one, but a journey less. I put out the call for woman who wanted to share their story of how they overcame something and discovered their worth. I had 15 to answer the call, only seven completed the task. Seven is the number of completion and I believe God has given me a variety of stories and testimonies that will inspire other women to share their journey. If you would be interested in being in volume two contact me: drhenderson77@gmail.com or 737-228-3207.

Through It All

By Selena Glenn

Where do I begin. Born to the parents of Charles and Carolyn Glenn on May 2, 1969. The first born of three, life was simple and looking good, that was before I learned what honor, pain, and abuse were. I want to say it was the mid-seventies when we moved from Tennessee to Los Angeles, California. I had to be about four years old. I do not remember much about that time, but I do remember my parents had a friend that was in a wheelchair who soon became my Godfather. Duce was a nice old me and I remember him telling me, "Shine your light, never let anybody take that beautiful smile from you." That smile soon would be taken away, and so was my worth.

Summer of 1974 my life changed forever I was only five years old when I was kidnapped from Venice Beach Playground, I was missing for five or six hours before I made my way back to my parents. I remember it like it was yesterday, from that day forward all my worth as I thought had been taken from me without my permission. I was innocent, but very aware of what had happened to me. I stayed to myself most of the time because I did not want any of the kids asking me any questions. I would just sit alone and stare at the sky. I was so young just a child, but I felt worthless like nobody loved me or ever would love me. How could they, I was damaged.

Two years later I'm seven and thought to myself, "Why was I treated so bad? I thought to myself the pain could not last forever.", but that was not the case. I can remember so vividly when I started first grade that we had moved to the hood and these kids were different from the kids I had been subject to. See Charles (Dad) was a military man and to top it off his mom was white, So, he did not see anything wrong with me not having black friends, but that changed, now I have a few friends and he did not like that. He did not like me having friends, because shortly after the Venice Beach incident, he started touching me.

Five years after, and I'm 11 and still going through the same thing, at this point I knew I would never be worthy of anything. How could it be when you hear your friends talk good about their upbringing, saying how much they parents loved them and would do anything for them. Not me, but one thing I did know, my mother loved me. She just had a very funny way of showing it. You will understand this later.

It was summer of 1979, my mom left with my little sister to go to the store my brother was outside playing, I was in my room by myself as usual. People in our apartment building had started talking and asking questions, because of the way I was acting, and the things I was saying was not normal for a kid my age. It wasn't, "How come I couldn't be like every other girl my age? Why was I going through so much at a very young age. I had witnessed seen, heard, and felt shit that I should not have.

Years later I'm now 16 in a gang, had been in a gang since I was twelve, joining a gang saved me from the monster I was living with. I'm in the 9th grade been kicked out of Lynwood High for gang banging now I'm at Wheaton Jr. High where I met his best friend, named Man. Man was a real cool guy, friendly, understanding and could not quit figure me out of class and hung behind the gym. So, one day after being disrespectful to our teacher Mr. Thomas he asked me, "Why? at this point?" I thought my life was not ever going to be any better. So, I tell Man everything that I had been through and was going through. For some reason I felt like I could trust him. So, I laid it all on the table. I told him everything he was so mad I had never seen anyone care about how I felt, but Man, did, that's the day I learned what being in a gang really meant. They had your back if you needed it and I was in need. Man told me," If he tries to touch you again, he will be dealt with." That's exactly what I did. You should have seen the fear in his eyes, he knew I wasn't playing.

Let me back up for a minute, he knew I could hurt him, because he used to beat on my mother, and I always was there to help her. Now if I could have killed him and got away with it, I would have. He put my mom through hell.

I remember being a kid and going to black magic places with her and her friends for rituals she could perform on him because he used to cheat and beat her like it was the thing to do. I can also remember when I was in like the 1st Grade and my mom used to hide me and my siblings in a closet that she had put a phone in because anytime he felt like tripping, he did. One night my mom knew he was going to come home on one, so she had already told us what to do just in case, and it went down just like she had known it would. As soon as we heard hi start fussing and cussing, Ronnie, Jason, John, and I eased out the back door and got in the car and locked the doors like my mom had said.

Now mind you it's in the 70's and we lived in Lynwood when there were not many blacks there. We were one of two black families that stayed on that street, but as my mom would say they were black, but not black. I didn't know what that meant then, but I do now, looking back she was right because their children weren't allowed to play with us. At the time I thought I wasn't worth or wasn't good enough to play with them.

Moving back to my gang banging days, yes that's when I knew my nightmare was over. I had my homies, I had made a name for myself in the hood, and my life was starting to change. My nightmare was over, but my hay days had just begun. I was banging and had a lot of friends. My secret was safe with Man, he was and still till this day is a great friend. I was so far from peace in my life. In 1985 I had my first son, in 1986 I had my second son, in 1988 I had my third son, in 1990 I had my fourth son and in 1991 I had my fifth son. By the time I was 25 I had five sons and felt and knew I would be worthy and loved by my sons. They were mine, and I would get love from them.

Unfortunately, my nightmare wasn't over because now I'm carrying my pain from my past into my relationships. I didn't know how to love because I really didn't know what love was. I loved my boys and I know my boys loved me, but other than that I had no clue how to love someone. My trust was gone. How could I trust what a man had to say when the one man who was supposed to love you unconditionally had hurt you for years and made you feel unworthy, I struggled for years on how to love my partner. As years went by, I would tell myself, "You got this, make the best of what you got." But that was never good enough for me, I wanted closure. I knew there was ither people who knew what went on with me as a child, but back in the 70's women just swept things under the rug and those who knew would just keep it a family secret, but we all know what goes on in the dark will come to the light. There's one person that can testify to everything I'm saying and that's my Auntie. I'll share a conversation we had.

Me: Some people are so sick in the head, and I always knew in my heart that something wasn't right, every time I asked about it, she would just brush me off.

Auntie: I hated how she treated you and Terrance (My brother) and felt like I wished I had been able to help you although I feared her and that gun she carried. I know it was totally useless now, but I feel sometimes like going to your mom with you and confronting her, but like you said she's sick and I guess it wouldn't do anything as this point.

Me: No, it wouldn't at all. All she's going to do is deny it and put me out. She puts me out all the time, all I must do is say something she doesn't like. Hell, I barely started coming back around and the only reason I did is because I knew she was not in the best of health, and someone had to look out for her. I just don't have that kind of hate in my soul. What I've been through in life makes me a strong woman, and plus at the end of the day she is the lady who gave me life.

Auntie: Well, you're a very good daughter Lovette because after all you've been through, most daughters would have said screw it and cut ties with her, but you've got a good heart even if she doesn't seem to appreciate it.

Me: Yes, Auntie I must visit because she treated me like I didn't belong my whole life I just couldn't set back and watch her waste away. You know I don't know my mom's side of the family? Last time I seen her mom I was eight years old. I have never met her sisters Julie and Faith. I only know Auntie Ruby and Auntie Jean. That's crazy huh, but I her other children know.

My pass haunts me all the time. Auntie, I just know how to deal with it by making the best in myself, when you grow up being told you're not shit, it was difficult to stay focused. But I had a friend named Jesus Christ, Jesus Christ our Savior, and He has never ever left my side. It's only because of Him I'm here today.

Auntie: I'm so glad. I wish I could have helped you get more.

Me: No problem auntie your back was up against the wall.

Auntie: I love you so much and I know you've been through living hell for what seems like most of your life.

Me: I love you to auntie all the pain I endured made me one strong ass woman.

Auntie: I remember you were always treated the worst and I absolutely hated that because you were my favorite, I just had wished that I had known what was going on because my being afraid of her back then would not have stopped me from getting you out of that house and getting custody of you myself. I am so sorry I didn't have any idea.

Me: I know you didn't know auntie; I don't hold it against you please believe me. She has issues. I used to think like; "what did I do," but it wasn't me, she was fighting her own demons. I catch myself sitting and crying all the time and I have to say, "Lovette, it's not your fault and look! You made it this far.

Auntie: Yes, I remember her emotional abuse and some physical, but she didn't let me witness much physical abuse maybe she thought I would call the authorities, I don't know but when I saw unexplained marks on you, she would say, you fell, and have you lie to me and tell me yes, I fell.

I remember that you were kind of a sad quiet child, but she always told me it was due to what happened at Vince Beach, I had no idea it was going on in your own home and that really pisses me off. I was abused by my uncle when I was a little girl, but my mom believed me and it stopped right away, but you never get over it and it affects your adult relationships with me later in life.

Through it all I'm still standing, and I know I am worth it. This is just the beginning stay tuned for the rest of the story.

Selena, my dear Selena, I thank you for trusting me with your story. Working two jobs and getting this done was a task, but you did what you have learned to do to become a woman of worth. You persevered and got it done. It took a lot of reminders, but you did it. I can only hope this will give you the confidence you need to continue.

Dr. Yvonne Henderson

Life is But a Dream…

By Tamela Funchess

I sat alone in the sterile, cold room, the crinkling sound of roll-out sanitary paper under my bottom, as I readjusted on the table. "I'm sorry Mrs. Funchess but your pregnancy test came back negative". These words had echoed in my ear once again. After many years trying to conceive, they had become way too familiar. It was another heartbreaking moment, and it stung.

I'd always dreamt of becoming a mother. Most girls dream of getting married and planning the perfect wedding. Marriage was never the end-goal. I just wanted to be a mother and knew I would be a great mom. I remember writing down all the names of my future children. So, once I hit my thirties and still found myself childless, devastated couldn't even describe how I felt. I recall speaking out loud that if I don't have a child by 35, I don't want it! Thankfully, God had His own timeline.

But first, let's explore the back story. My childhood home, while I didn't fully understand it at the time, was tumultuous. We had good times, but my parent's marriage was toxic. It was abusive, and it left scares. Any situation could randomly sour. From my perspective, we could be having an ordinary day, and suddenly, a dark cloud would appear in the form of anger. This caused a lot of unresolved anxiety and uncertainty that wouldn't manifest until years later. Around the time I turned 8, my mom finally found the courage to leave. I remember it vividly. She picked my sister and I up early from school, car packed to the ceiling. We drove away and never looked back. That should've been a great knew beginning, however, it was the start of new struggles and new challenges.

The trauma of my parents' marriage left my mom broken and without much to give to her children. If you've ever been in an abusive relationship, you know that once you leave that environment, while the physical abuse is no longer there, the scares run deep and can have long lasting effects. Once we left, I watched her struggle to keep a roof over our heads and food on the table. I didn't have words for it at the time, but I now know that she was hurting. Substances abuse, her coping method, pushed her further away. It not only pushed us away from her, but consequently, pushed my sister and I away from each other.

Like many from my generation, I did not have a positive example of what love, or a healthy relationship looked like. All I knew was I wanted, no, needed my mother to mother me, and she didn't have the capacity. It was during those years that I decided that being a mother would be my greatest joy.

Just imagine the sting of watching my 20's, 30's roll away and not being able to conceive. I had a couple of long-term relationships prior to getting married, so it wasn't for the lack of opportunity. Looking back, however, I am so grateful that none of those relationships produced a child. Trust, it would have been a nightmare. Thank God that HE knew what was best for me because I had not a clue.

At 23 and months away from graduating college, I met my now husband. While I wanted a child, I still wasn't mentally or emotionally ready to be a mom. You know how sometimes you can want something that you think is perfect for you and then look back years later to realize you dodged a bullet? Yeah, it was like that. How would I be able to provide stability and love for a child when I was still trying to figure ME out?

I had witnessed other young women struggle to take care of children they were unprepared for. Even though I felt some type of way, I knew that I didn't want that to be my story. Stability for my child was non-negotiable. Something I never had.

I dated my husband for 5 years prior to getting married. I must admit, we faced many challenges during that time. Being young and immature and being honest, I wasn't ready for a serious relationship. I didn't know or understand what being in a real relationship entailed. All I knew was looking out for self.

Past trauma had me vulnerable. I wasn't thinking clearly, and from the "single mother" hustle mentality I was raised in, I saw my husband as my current opportunity versus a real thing. That mindset caused a lot of riffs in our relationship, and I will own that part. He was "raised", I "grew-up". He was ready, I wasn't. It was a time, trust me.

While our relationship had many red flags, we still decided to wed. By this time, I was approaching 30 and ready to have a baby. IT WAS NOT HAPPENING! At first, we were casually trying, and then it became more urgent.

We underwent medical tests and protocols to help us conceive, but nothing worked. I felt so low. I remember not being able to enjoy intimacy because I felt like an empty hole. The emotional turmoil of it all is still real. I had gotten to the point where I was like, what's the point? Why just let this man take pleasure in my body when the results I was hoping for seemed impossible? It was a dark time.

If you have never experienced infertility, it's hard to explain. It is very isolating, very numbing. I was spiraling into a depression. We did have our church family and faith to lean on, but at the time, it just wasn't enough. Nothing could bring me joy. I spent a significant amount of time not truly living my life or enjoying my marriage due to being consumed with what I wanted. Looking back, I know I missed out on my opportunities to create memories. It's like a blur. Years I cannot reclaim.

It was so bad. I remember telling my husband that if we don't have children, I did not want to be married. I felt like if we were not able to create a family, what was the point of being attached? I figured, if I couldn't become a mother, I would rather be single and operate in my freedom. Think, rich auntie vibes.

Depression kicked my butt. Now that I'm thinking about it, I didn't realize I was depressed. It showed up as overindulging in alcohol, smoking, partying, and not taking care of myself. The worse times would be the holiday season. I would dread the holidays. People spending time with their children, making the holidays special for them. It was all just too much. I can recall a few years I chose not to participate in the holidays. I just couldn't stomach it.

Then, one year, EVER THING changed. It was like a lightbulb came on and the darkness started to clear. It started with a Daniel fast with our church. My husband and I were drinking, smoking, and eating horribly at the time. When the fast was announced, we were like, ok, we can do this. I don't know exactly what it was, but I knew it was time for a change, a shift, a new season. We successfully completed the 21 days, extended it to 40, and eventually it grew into significant life changes.

Taking control of our lives, we started eating better, trusting God more and even joined a gym. It was an exciting time. While I had still not conceived, the weight of it was much lighter, literally. I began to feel better, look better, and be better. I finally surrendered and made peace with not having children. I just wanted to, no NEEDED to enjoy my life, this life. The one that was childfree yet blessed.

We became the poster couple of transformation. Everyone wanted to know what we were doing and how we were doing it. Even our doctors had questions. Prior to this, my husband's urologist had ordered an expensive procedure for him to endure. We declined. While my infertility was "unexplained", his doctor seemed to think that varicose veins in testicles may have been the problem. After changing our lifestyle, he went for a follow-up visit and his doctor was surprised to learn that whatever issue he had, had resolved itself. That was a green flag moment for us.

For the first time in a long time, I was, dare I say "happy". The wave lasted for a while, but I would still find myself with the nagging feeling that I was missing something from my life. My energy focus had shifted, but I still longed to be a mother. The blessed part about it was that I wanted it but wasn't stressed over it. I was content.

My annual doctor appointments became easier to handle. I wasn't expecting to hear I was pregnant, so it didn't hurt as much. I remember going in for my routine check-up and my doctor, who had been with me the whole time, asked was I still trying to conceive. By this time, I was 35. I politely said, "no, it's too late". She rebuked that comment and convinced me to try one last thing. She referred me to an endocrinologist who I was to see immediately.

Reluctantly, I made an appointment and went in. He did all the things, asked all the questions, ran all the test, and then prescribed a series of pills that I was to being taking on day 5 of my next menstrual cycle. I wasn't very optimistic, but I agreed to try. One thing that stood out from that appointment though, was when he did an ultrasound, he told me that my uterine lining was very thin and asked if it was time for my cycle. It was that time, so he didn't think anything of it.

Every day after that appointment, I waited for my period to start. It didn't. Instead of thinking I could be pregnant, my thoughts were, here we go again. I have something that may be able to help me but now my body is acting funny. Life went on. I'll never forget. It was spring break, was off work, and I was celebrating.

Days later, during a typical gym session, I noticed that I was feeling very weak and fatigued. It was unusual because I had been working out for a while at this point. I was in great shape! I remember calling my husband from the gym to tell him how I was feeling. He spoke words that I have never heard pass his lips. He said, "you should take a pregnancy test". I was taken back. In my mind, how I felt, and pregnancy test did not have a connection.

Once I got home, I went ahead and took a test. Just to prove him crazy...I peed on the stick, sat it on the counter, and jumped in the shower. I had zero expectations, just appeasing him. Stepping out of the shower, my mind was not on the test. Afterall, why would I be concerned about another negative result? Once I got out, I saw it, picked it up, read "positive", and nearly fell out. I immediately started screaming, "Hell nah! Hell nah!" I ran into the living room, dripping wet, screaming, and carrying on. My husband didn't know what was happening.

As I held up the test stick, I was shouting, "what does this say!?!?" He took it from my hand and looked at it. I just recall an unexplainable expression coming over his face. He was shocked and maybe a little confused. He shouted, "you're pregnant!"

You know what we did next, right? We took several more tests to confirm it wasn't a fluke. We were tripping, tripping! Once the excitement settled, we both looked happy, confused, dazed, and, admittedly, scared. It was an interesting moment. I was excited, but at the same time, I was like, "who will be friends with our child?" All our friend's children were teenagers. "Oh my! I'm going to be an old mom!" It was quite the comical conversation I was having in my head.

The next day, I tried making an appointment with my OB/GYN. Per usual, she did not have any available appointments until a couple of weeks out. I couldn't wait. I made an appointment with a local clinic to confirm, and it was a YES! Oh My Gosh! It was a YES!

I must have taken a pregnancy test every day after that just to confirm and reconfirm. After a while, it became negative. I was scared. I found out though, that after a certain period, the pregnancy hormone no longer registered on the test. LOL! Who knew?

Now the question became, who would we tell first? We told my mom first, over a breakfast date. Then we shared the news with my dad via an Easter card for a grandpa, and finally, during the prayer for Easter dinner with my in-laws, we shared it with them. Everyone was so excited. It was so surreal. And what do you know? As fate had it, our niece announced her pregnancy that same night! Bingo, our baby has their first cousin/friend.

I took good care of myself during the entire pregnancy. I was still hitting the gym, not as hard. I ate well and rested as needed. It was a smooth pregnancy, no morning sickness, no major swelling, it was great. I became a first-time mom at the tender age of 36! Remember when I told God that if I don't have a child be 35, I didn't want one? Tuh...

It was during this time that I began to make the connection between wellness and thriving. Before this, I had never associated how I treat my body, what I put in my body, how I manage stress and how I care for myself overall, correlated to healthy outcomes. I trusted and relied on my black, female gynecologist to lead me and, even though I was overweight and unhealthy, she never spoke with me about wellness.

NEVER! As I think about it now, it's crazy. I won't say that this experience made me lose faith in the healthcare system, but it did alter my perspective.

My experience stirred up something in me. It birthed the idea of becoming a wellness coach and helping other women change their mindsets, change their lives, through wellness. Revitalize Me was born. Well, I wasn't calling it that at the time, but the idea was the same.

I went on to pursue a certification as a wellness coach and educate myself on wellness strategies to help transform lives from the inside out. Now, as a seasoned teacher of 19 years, my mission is the same, yet my focus has expanded. I'm working to bring awareness to the importance of wellbeing for educators. I work with women and educators teaching them strategies to help revive a sense of fulfillment both personally and professional via coaching, wellness workshops, and experiences.

Remember when I mentioned before that the holidays were the hardest times for me? Well, God is so good, he not only said He would restore my joy, He showed out in a major way. My one and only child was born during the Thanksgiving season. In fact, as I write this, her 10th birthday is approaching and lands on Thanksgiving Day this year. God is an awesome God.

To any woman who can relate to my story, any woman who has or is currently suffering from infertility, I stand with you. If you find yourself yet waiting on your blessing, my first piece of advice is to LET IT GO! That's right, I said let it go. Let go the pressure and stress you are putting on yourself and likely your relationship. Let go of the all-consuming thoughts. Let go and LIVE! Live the life you want NOW. Don't trap yourself in thoughts of what could be. Live in the moment with the faith that what is meant, shall be. I had to let go to receive. The stress I was putting on myself blocked me from conceiving, I am convinced of this. The unhealthy habits, the depression, the lack of self-care, all contributed to my issues. As soon as I decided to surrender, the impossible became reality.

As for the mother I've always wanted to be. I am living that dream. My daughter is the light of my life. I spend a lot of time and energy cultivating our relationship. Teaching her the lessons I wish I had been taught. Affording her the family environment I longed to have. Although I was only blessed with one child, I am eternally grateful. She is growing up so quickly, so beautifully, right before our eyes. I silently mourn her not being my "baby" anymore yet overjoyed watching her blossom and bloom into the rich, beautiful flower she is becoming.

She has taught me so much about life, about myself, and about unconditional love. She inspires me to continue to make wellness a priority, not only for myself, but for our family. She watches everything I do. As a result, I strive to be better each day. She sees me make good food choices, exercise, and practice self-care. We practiced meditation, breathing, and stretching together. Because of her, one of the greatest life changes my husband and I have recently made as parents was breaking up with alcohol.

I noticed that I had gotten back into the habit of drinking regularly. So often, that whenever we would go out for dinner, a drink would be the first thing I ordered. I recall, the waitress bringing my big, colorful drink to the table. My daughter looks at me and says, "that is pretty, can I taste it?" She had asked what I was drinking before, and I would also say a mommy drink or just wine. But this time, when she asked to "taste" it, I knew I had to give it up.

I am pleased to say that my husband and I are going on a year alcohol free, and it has been great. Not only has it improved my personal life, but it has made me a better, more effective coach. I mean, how can I promote wellness if I'm operating in unhealthy ways? It lets me know I am on the right path and the best is yet to come.

I am a Revitalization Coach, that is my superpower!

Take Charge of Creating the Life You Want While Enjoying the Life You Have.

Tamela, our stories are so similar. I am so glad you decided to share it. It's a story that a lot of women face and never share. It is a story that will inspire women everywhere who may want to have a child. The struggle is real, and the remedy may not always be from the medical field.

Dr. Yvonne Henderson

The Irony Life

By Dr. Barbara Bracy

When we think about LIFE, we don't really think about how it's going to be or how it was to be, we just let it play out. When you're born you have parents, guardians, or relatives. You have no control over who or what you get. Which in some cases could be considered the first irony of life that we face. Whoever has their hands on you for growth kind of decides which direction they want you to go, but if you don't go in that direction, then what. First, it may take you a lifetime to even recognize that there are ironies in life let alone your own. We don't have a hand on it, but they are there.

I often think that LIFE, yes, I am hollering at you. Is like a musical instrument, you live it, you learn it. It's like a practiced learned behavior that continues. I can only reflect on my life, and I can look around and peer down or up on other people's lives who have passed through my life. I give all thanks to God, for keeping me and bringing me this far. Even me writing this chapter is ironic, I would have never thought in a million years I would be writing a chapter in an anthology, but as the ironies of life would have it, I am here writing it.

I was raised by two parents, or should I say, I was thought of by two people that when they laid down to make love, decided they wanted a child, or was willing to accept the outcome of a child. I was wanted, I was loved. In fact, I was given so much love, I think I rushed their time of death, not me, I didn't rush it, however my time with them, because it was such a short span with me. My father died when I was 21 and my mother died when I was 30 maybe 35. The way they lived has left such an impression on me. The irony of life was my dad was an attorney and my mom worked at a state hospital and I was an only child, I had a sister, but she lived in another state. I was the only child in the household. The freedom and love that they gave me was so overlapping and extensive that the irony of them being taken away from me at such an early stage in my life was hard to grasp. What they left me with, I sponged off for the rest of my life.

Oh the ironies of life, and I'm sure you or others can think of things in your life that maybe one person said or did, it didn't have to be their parents it just happened to be my parents, it just happened to be the short time they were with me, that was so impactful that even in death I had a lot to carry on my back, in my heart, in my soul and, from the bottom of my feet, I had a lot to carry. Oh, the ironies of life. So, when you pay attention or a made to pay attention to things you begin to wonder, why are things as they are and what would happen, if they were not this way.

Oh, the ironies of life. I remember a first cousin of mine died early and other things, my uncles and cousins, one after another, my family left very early and I stopped one day and told God, "You got my attention," I had to be made a believer, I think the irony of my freedoms and the impact of the love that I was given, "How could this be happening?" I had to be made a believer and so being obedient unbeknownst to what I was being, maybe I would say the learned practice behavior that you are constantly involved with makes us become believers. God was, and whatever their number was, and the day, it had come. Whatever the reason the people were leaving, they were leaving.

Most people's families are brought together by marriage or happens stance, but my relatives, and ironically from the same hometown. My mother's people and my father's people knew each other. My uncle was in the same classroom that my mother's first cousin was in. My mother and father knew each other when they were younger, maybe high school because that was where I heard the most stories. When my mother and dad's family would get together, it was ironic, because they all knew each other, and it seemed like one big happy family. It was also ironic how my uncle on my dad's side was married to my mother's friend, who I thought was my blood aunt on her side of the family, but she was my aunt because she married my dad's brother, the ironies of life.

It is also ironic when things are twisted and turned and turned and twisted, it gives you time to reflect, even if you don't want to. The ironies of life whether they come in this situation, or not they will impact you, whether you recognize it or not., I don't know if you will even want to read this, but I just wanted to share how when this thing called LIFE, in capital letters, yes yelling at you, it goes full circle, it's like you're born, you make steps, you continue to grow and grow and grow, then you're right back where you started. It's said that if you live long enough you will revert "Once an adult, twice a child." I've seen it with the elderly. Oh, The irony of life.

Dr. Bracy, for our paths to cross again after some ten years is not an accident. The last time we collaborated was while we worked on our dissertations. It is a blessing to have you be a part of my first anthology. Talk about the irony of life. Thank you for your contribution to this collection. Your words will resonate with more than you would probably imagine.

Dr. Yvonne Henderson

Driven and Free

By Tanya J. Haynes

Starting the Engine

During the summer, I presented professional development for a group of librarians, and it was electrifying. During the first week, I shared many good tips and tricks I had learned throughout my years in librarianship, and it felt so good. I was able to "rise to the moment" like a visiting minister reminded us during a Sunday morning message. I was blessed to have this opportunity to help others by sharing my professional learnings and experiences, but the road to the race began by getting in the car and starting the engine.

As an educator first and a librarian second, my goal has always been and always will be to develop students' intellect. Yes, students need academic knowledge in all subject areas, but they also need to know how much you care about them as a person before you present the just right book or the informational website or the perfect author. After many years in the classroom, I returned to graduate school to earn a master's in library information science; initially, I thought the library would be a better place for me, tired of bringing work home, especially reading all the essays. It was too much. I desired time for myself again and time with my family. In my forties, I returned to school and finished earning my degree walking across the stage as an example to our son. This was no easy feat; lifelong learning takes you off the curb and centers you on the main street.

Initially, my first campus as a librarian was stupendous; I landed a secondary librarian position at a middle school. I recall the interview; I 'nailed' it. As I was driving down Highway 6 on my way home; the principal called my cell phone to tell me she was so excited and wanted to offer me the position, but she couldn't officially do that, so I should be expecting a call from the Human Resources department soon. I celebrated. I was delivered from grading papers. I enjoyed each day getting to know the staff and working diligently to form collaborative networks with each subject area department leader.

I also worked to change the culture of reading at the school; unfortunately, this middle school was not known for its academics and students struggled with comprehension therefore they did not enjoy reading. My goal as a first-year librarian was to change that and usher in a new age of librarianship. Quickly, I learned that the library was not a well thought of area of the school; most often it is forgotten. With the 'hustle and bustle' of raising test scores to improve the school's rating, the library is often overlooked as not a primary department. My job as a new-age librarian was to change that, so my focus was two-fold.

First, I generated excitement about reading by making it fun to do with the start of my genre-based lunchtime book club called Triple T Reading, Takin' Time to Read. We met monthly; kids loved it. Because I had a budget, I was able to buy items for the monthly themes. Although I don't like scary books, every good librarian knows students love them, so one month I bought decorations and games and students walked in the library at lunch time in awe of the dramatic change of the decor and the set up. They chose their own chair to sit and eat and talk to their peers about the scary book they had read. Realizing that all students did not read the book or finished the book was alright because Triple T gave students the push, they needed to explore their reading lives. Students came month after month stoked to have a good time and see what Mrs. Haynes had in store for them. This campus had lunch for 6th graders, 7th graders, and 8th graders, so we repeated three different book clubs on the same day each month. It was lively; and the reading culture began to change that very first year.

Secondly, I generated monthly reports advocating for the crucial work the library was doing on behalf of changing the reading culture with striving readers; the data from book circulations, and other events hosted by the library and happenings in the space vital to other departments to improving student achievement drives home the importance of this often-forgotten department. The emailed report was disseminated in the form of a Microsoft PowerPoint to each of the teachers and administrators; it also contained images from the book club meeting, process of upgrading the collection, collaborative efforts with teachers, and how budget dollars aided their classroom instruction in the form of technology and other resources.

Geared Up

Educators and other professionals treasured a welcoming, warm library too. At the beginning of the school year, my priority was setting up class visitations, as I was on a flexible schedule, ordering books that teachers needed to supplement curriculum, checking out technology devices for teachers use in the classroom, and giving adults a brief library orientation, so that they understood the inner workings of library and all the services afforded to them during the school year from collaborative efforts to student library programming to literacy events.

I found myself always having a kind, uplifting word to all those who passed through the library doors. At one campus, I used a beautiful box I purchased from Hobby Lobby; it looked like a book, but one side opened. I printed bible scripture verses and other inspirational quotes on paper and cut them into slips and folded them.

The motivation box always sat on the library's circulation desk so teachers and other staff members could quickly receive an inspired word to start their day or to continue their day or to end their day. There were countless testimonies from colleagues who said they always received the right note for the right moment. Their words always uplifted me to know God was using me in a manner I did not expect. Each of us needs to be reminded about the truth that lies with us; and we can and will make it even in those darkest moments. I always took joy in selecting the quotes, but I also purchased colorful stickers, sparkly stickers and other accents to comfort people.

During my tenure at this intermediate campus, the library was literally the center of the school dividing one grade level from the other grade level. With close to 1,500 students in fifth and sixth grades, most students would be considered growing (or reluctant) readers, so I engaged students in multiple formats to encourage them as human beings first, individually, and collectively. This enabled me to provide avenues for students to read for pleasure and talk about reading with their peers.

Shifting gears in my professional learning allowed my librarianship skills to grow and I was able to impact this school's reading culture as well in multiple ways. I changed lanes from viewing books and budget as the only road to reading achievement to steering students and adults to high quality library programming constructed to grow striving readers up the road of life-long learning. The school's community desired not only great books to read but regular intervals of learning activities. Makerspace learning was trending in the national library world, but how could I get this knowledge of this type of hands-on learning out of the pit-stop of my brain into the main lanes of the school.

Morning Library rolled on Mondays. Wednesdays, and Fridays from 7:50 a.m. - 8:20 a.m. Students had many choices from computer time games to building makers to robotic makers to silent reading and book renewals and/or checkout of new books. The students' response was amazing and overwhelming. Originally, makerspaces were open on first come, first served, but due to large student response and the library capacity holding only 75 students at one time I had to rework the entry starting point. So, homeroom teachers were giving one pass to distribute to a most deserving student to attend Morning Makerspaces each week. Teachers were encouraged to give different students a chance from week to week. Daily students formed a line to enter the library for makers' fun and two teachers earned supplemental paid for monitoring students and facilitating activities.

One side of the library was dedicated to the student news team prepping for the school's morning broadcast. The instructional technology specialist trained and monitored those four to five students. At a few tables on that same side, a few silent readers sat enjoying their books. In the center of the library, approximately twelve desktops were regularly used by students for learning games and projects. The noise was intense; the library isn't always a quiet place as some believe. Learning can be noisy, fun, and thrilling. The center tables were dedicated to board games and creative drawing and coloring. The final third of the library housed the building makerspaces including KEVA planks. The library should never be a one event show, if the space is made for more. Our library hosted a few activities and events regularly and simultaneously. It was a smooth ride until the pandemic and then I shifted gears again and the library continued the joyride.

Emergency Brake

My last campus took me for a major detour although the route was beautiful and scenic in the beginning. After leaving my previous district in hopes of a new position, I found myself at a school library that was in a head-on collision with mismanagement and years of hoarding. I interviewed and accepted the position online without seeing the school or the library. When I finally saw the library, I cried for two days in my bedroom on the floor in the dark; it was just that bad. I am always blessed to clean up others' mess because I do such an outstanding job. After crying, I reset my mind and started the work, and it was a lot of work. The library had technology all over it: computer carts, boxes of keyboards, clear containers of classroom technology. The library's workroom had several carts of books needing to be cataloged, the unorganized cabinets had years and years' worth of items, and two of the additional rooms had books and other items that needed to be decluttered and organized. After cleaning and reorganizing the entire library, it was finally presentable for staff and students.

During the initial year, I also started two book clubs which students did not have access to previously. Soaring Eagles Book Club permitted struggling readers opportunities to read on their grade level and talk about the books while Texas Bluebonnet Book Club was geared at on level and advanced readers. During the mornings, club members meet biweekly to discuss their books and complete coordinated activities while eating donuts and kolaches. Students loved the book clubs, and the principal was impressed at the championship style changes made in my first year. Our school board's foundation awarded my grant and the library received funds for the gentrification process: both fiction and non-fiction books were gentrified by categories and topics by the end of the school year. During my end of the year elevation, the principal stated she did not think that much progress could be made in such a short amount of time.

Mid-way through my second year on campus, the master schedule was adjusted to include the library as a special class, so instead of seeing students' kindergarten through 2nd grade once a week and third through fifth grade the next week on a rotating basis students rode into the largest classroom every day. The fixed schedule roared in, and I taught lessons to kindergarten through fifth grade daily. The principal, the content specialists, the specials team, and the teachers were very pleased. Although I experienced the pros and cons of the fixed schedule, I was learning to adjust and settle into my new wheels. Then, I was told to give each student a music participation grade. Everything shrieked to a stop!

As a Texas certified school librarian primary through twelfth grades, lifetime Louisiana sixth through twelfth grades English Language Arts Reading (ELAR) teacher, and Texas eighth through twelfth grades ELAR, Speech, and English as a Second Language (ESL) teacher, I did not feel comfortable assigning music grades (a subject for which I am not certified) a grade. Firstly, I did not think that would be an honest assessment of the literacy work students were involved in in the library especially since I did not get a clear answer as to whether parents were notified of this class modification.

Finally, and most importantly, my instructional engine ran steadily for the tremendous asset of the library's ability to pivot for students in the absence of a certified music teacher; however, the official record of the library advancing the students towards the campus' finish line to win this learning race would never be recognized. As the library's leader that was extremely unsettling. This grading difference acted as a catalyst to my next adventure.

Revved Up

Deciding to take a leap of faith I resigned from my elementary librarian position. Because I was hurting and stressed, I knew others had to be feeling similar emotions and God was leading me to help myself as well as other professionals. So, I turned the proverbial corner, and packed up all my items. Like teachers, most librarians invest a lot of their own personal finances in the library to make it the most desirable space for the community. After packing, I submitted my letter of resignation to the principal a few days before the end of the school year. My hope was to give the administrators ample time to find a good librarian; the students need a librarian who could meet their academic needs.

The main professional road led me to an unexpected curve; I "launched out into the deep" as I encouraged other ladies to do when I acted as mistress of ceremony at the church's ladies conference. After twenty-five in education as a teacher and specialized teacher, librarian, I found myself on a new street in a totally unfamiliar territory. In Luke 5, Simon Peter and other disciples worked tirelessly throughout the night trying to catch fish but had no success until after following Jesus' command. Year after year, I followed the road laid out for most Americans. Go to school, get good grades, earn the degree, and get a "big job" like my mother-in-law once said. But the promotion did not come even when I worked hard and waited patiently and kept my 'head down' and worked even harder, in fact not only did the promotion not come but my fire was doused with water year after year, project after project, and detour after detour and it left me with a little spark.

At the word of my Father, I started Fiya Librarian Consulting, LLC in July 2023, so now I drive my own car. Although my car is not a Bentley, I am grateful for the ride. This vehicle rolls in new opportunities to share my journey with other educators, teachers, professionals, and anyone who will listen. In my sharing, I can assist others to build literacy in their local communities with the library as the pit stop where individuals of all ages find their own vehicles and drive their own learning as the library acts as a flare lighting the way for future learning for other generations.

My initial net was cast this summer when I served as a facilitator in my test run presenting original content created in my three-year plan for professional development for librarians, educators, and staff. During my trial run, I was able to invite an emerging local author and budding educational entrepreneur in collaborative workshops highlighting picture books and learning binders as valuable resources for students. In addition to workshops, the specialized three-hour sessions engaged teachers, librarians, and other literacy professionals about the roles of libraries and work of librarians. The favorable feedback helps build more highways for the newly started company.

Revising my business plan prepares me to cast another net in the upcoming year. As the net goes deeper in another section of water, Fiya Librarian gains additional knowledge through networking to take in additional fish. Early next year my Minority/Women Owned Business Enterprise certifications should be approved by its authorizing agency and Fiya Librarian's goal to benefit public librarians and staff will be realized. The literacy model, more bait, is the final part of the plan ready to cast on the water next year. Our earliest ancestors worked demanding and exhausting lives and coveted communicative skills like reading and writing, then future ancestors frustrated by past erroneous views contended and debated for equality. Current generations may forge valiantly ahead using The Fiya Literacy™ Model which encompasses families and educators working harmoniously together to leave a legacy of learning.

Even during my summer vacation bible school adventures, we were indoctrinated with the foundational principle that the Word of God reigns supreme. The Word of God is the ultimate training manual guiding people into eternity. My vacation bible school class taught us that the bible encompasses "basic instructions before leaving earth". Recently, as a facilitator of the Christian Education webinar for church leaders, I was able to share sound biblical instructional strategies innate to constructing settings conducive to educating the whole student–natural and spiritual. For additional reading materials, view my blog encouraging teachers to Get in Place; our Sunday School classes need you. Students need to know how to 'connect the information dots' in this digital world because knowledge is plentiful, but everything is not true; students and adults need to think critically about the information received from all resources whether friends, teachers, parents, or the church.

So, editing my business model to include digital products aimed at character and Christian education removes the barriers of separation of church and state because students need a strong foundation rooted in biblical principles. The biblical foundation removes the roadblocks set by current political ideology and restores some ideals in which this country was founded.

Now, I dedicate my days seeking the open roads paved for Fiya Librarian Consulting, LLC through the people God has ordained for this company to positively affect. In the public schools, I encouraged others through kind words and inspirational scriptures as often as possible but had to take a backstreet when comforting students through the Word of God. If a student stated he went to church or prayed over his food at lunch time, I considered that an open road to drive right in, but now there is no brake. Fiya Librarian Consulting travels all lanes open to God and encourages others to do the same before the inevitable crash of their life.

    A few months ago, my husband came home, and he said, "I like this new Tanya; she's driven and free". She is focused, confident, and full of Holy Ghost and fire. If the roads you travel on are under construction or closed, and you are looking for a new lane, revisit your navigation. Take the ramp to positive thoughts. Leave the past in your rear-view mirror. Make a pit stop by the house of God to gas up your vehicle with premium information fuel regularly. Set your vehicle on cruise control to your nearest library. Let's drive; let's go!

Tanya, you have given me a different outlook on librarians. I, like many others probably do not realize how important you all are to the educational process. Thanks to your passion and your program, schools can and will be changed forever. Thank you for using this platform to release your story.

Dr. Yvonne Henderson

To God Be The Glory!

By Jessica Lockett

I was born on August 26, 1983; to a single mother that was born in 1944; was raised in Louisiana. I am an only child, and I had a beautiful childhood, when it came to holidays and birthdays. My mom and dad divorced when I was around four or five years old. I only have two memories of my father and they were not good ones. My dad was something we did not talk about, and I was not allowed to ask questions. The few instances I did my mother earnestly refused to discuss him. It was very painful for her. I did not understand why I could not see or talk to my father. There were just some things that were not discussed. Knowing what I know now it is understandable. The pain was too much to relive.

Growing up I was very timid and went along with the flow, that's the best way I can describe it. I was terrified to ask or do anything that would get me yelled at. I can remember my insecurities started around age 9, I had acne, was skinny, and had low self-esteem, while struggling in school. From 4th grade to 12th school was beginning to be harder and harder. You would probably find that hard to believe with an educator for a parent, but even with those resources I did just enough to get by and graduate from high school. No, college was not on my agenda or in my future.

I found out I was pregnant. My boyfriend proposed to me Christmas night, 2001, I didn't except the proposal and soon after broke up. This was the beginning of a cycle that I wasn't ready for. I graduated in 2002 at 17 pregnant with my daughter. In 2009, I gave birth to my son by another man. In 2013, I had my third child, and then my baby girl was born in 2016. It wasn't until a friend of mine said" that I was in relationship after relationship and by the age of 31 I had a total of 4 children by 3 different men. Jessica, you have had a child in every relationship you have, somethings not right with that." I quickly realized I had never addressed my struggles and low-self-esteem image.

I attempted to create a life with my two youngest daughter's dad. I had what I thought a family was and did what I thought I should as a mom, and partner/mate. I found myself in a toxic relationship that put me and my children in harm's way. I wanted to leave, but it became difficult because shortly after having my last child I became very sick, and my health began to spiral downward. My relationship was very abusive both mentally and physically. I stayed in this relationship for years! My children witnessed relentless arguments and physical abuse. I had hit rock bottom; I didn't know what to do or who I was.

Soon God revealed what I was going through reflected how I thought about myself. All the pain, sickness and loss were the results of the truth I had to accept; I didn't Love myself let alone know myself.

My firstborn daughter ran away from home because of the environment we were in... I surrendered to God; I was at ground zero. When I chose to become better because I was fed up with my life, God stepped in! One night I said, "It's time, I fled for my life with my children in a car that had no gas. No, literally it was on "E", but I know it was only the grace of God that allowed us to make it out. I can recall my son saying, "Mommy look! Do you see that?" I didn't know what he was talking about because I was moving so fast. I looked, he said," Do you see the angles?" There were angels beside my car, and I knew then that God had me.

I had to accept that I didn't know how to or knew what love really was. Through me committing to God, and his Word. I engulfed myself in the Bible. The scriptures began to speak and heal my soul, I was becoming more aware of how I had been living verses, who God created me to be. I had fully accepted that I didn't love or know myself, and if I didn't know or love me. How could I give the love I needed to my children?

I confessed (wrote) about everyone and everything that had ever upset me. I had to Forgive.

Me and my children started affirming every day and to each other "I AM SMART, I AM LOVED, I AM UNIQUE, I COULD DO ANYTHING THAT I PUT MY MIND TO, etc.". After our affirmations we would paten it with scriptures (God's signature). Talk about a game changer! My family immediately started to heal and receive the counseling, help we needed.

Looking back at my journey I had to get to the root of what caused my demise. The foundation that I had to build life on was broken. I was raised by a strong black woman who was a college graduate, successful teacher, and so much more, who was striving through life with a broken heart. As God started to peel my layers back, providing me with understanding of what happens when you don't heal from a trauma or a traumatic situation. Without dealing/healing with something that hurts a person to the core. We hurt everyone and everything that comes our way, UNINTENTIONALLY.

I had been thirsty for love! Love that my mom thought she was giving. Not realizing that, she made a lot of her decisions based on the fear she had, from not dealing with her pain. The most mportant part of Life's journey is the foundation we begin from. Accepting the fact that I didn't Love myself and didn't know what love was, has been a truth (confession) that has landed me in this beautiful moment in time. Sharing with you. To God be the glory!

Jessica, oh Jessica, the first time meeting you was a divine connection. The stories we have shared and the obstacles we have faced together have been amazing, but your story, my love, has an empowerment all its own. Thank you for trusting me and stepping out of your comfort zone to share a piece of you with the world.

Dr. Yvonne Henderson

My Cross of Leadership
By Erica Bennett

*Mingled words,
lying tongues,
false hands,
wrong motive,
fallen moments,
darkened nights,
silent tears,
sleepless nights,
early mornings,
deep groanings,
bare bodied,
soul gripping
cross bearing,
fire refined.
hopeful smiles,
passion rise,
this cross I bear,
is mine alone.
this journey I take,
I walk it alone.
and out of the smoke,
and out of the shame,
and out of the abyss,
newness arise,
stripped, emptied, ready for healing.*

Welcome to my cross story, with so much to say, and not enough space. Let me begin by telling you that I cringe every time people ask, "what do you do?" I pause a little, due to the grandeur pretention that leadership titles and positions have on our awe-struck culture of glitter and shine. Therefore, in my testimony, I hope to implore all from the mountain top, that there is a cost and a cross of leadership that one must bear as they embark on their journey. And at our deepest and most fragile moments, the different faces of who you are, and public perception will war with your faith.

How it started

My bout with leadership started at an early age. From the age of 10 years old, I've learned the art of studying, reading, thinking, organizing, communicating, and presenting in a missionary Baptist church. Memorizing bible verses coupled with learning about our black history was a common theme. As a youth, I regularly led and engaged with student organizations in my church, school and community. Keep in mind, as an 80's baby, I was raised and trained by baby boomers who were active in civil rights, business, and public service organizations in which they had to fight for the right to have a seat at the table, any table, in any industry. Being taught how to achieve and strive despite resistance echoed in the training I received growing up. One of the blessings and curses of being a black woman in our country is that we were taught and trained that if we wanted to achieve success, we would have to work harder than everyone else, get a college degree, and set yourself apart as one of the best. This mindset coursed through my blood and moved with every lock and step of my being.

I read and proclaimed inspirational thoughts and quotes of leadership, endurance, and greatness from some of the greatest minds of our nation. Studying the life of Harriet Tubman, Ida B. Wells, Sojourner Truth, and many others became my hobby. Soaking up various thoughts of liberation, education and success enriched my very essence. Here are a few quotes that I have meditated on below:

- "For I am my mother's daughter, and the drums of Africa still beat in my heart. They will not let me rest while there is a single Negro boy or girl without a change to prove his worth,'" by Mary McLeod Bethune (Johnson, 1995).
- "Women, if the soul of the nation is to be saved, I believe you must become its soul," by Coretta Scott King (Johnson, 1995).
- "People don't pay much attention to you when you are second best. I wanted to see what it felt

like to be number one," Florence Griffith Joyner (Johnson, 1995).
- "Education is the jewel casting brilliance into the future," Mari Evans (Johnson, 1995).

Those inspirational words moved within me a passion to help others in various aspects of life. Scholastics, curiosity, ambition, and the desire to serve moved my feet. When I majored in education in college, I simultaneously studied and looked for work-based experiences in writing, journalism, business, public service, and non-profit work due to my desire to make a positive impact on those I serve.

In hindsight, the way I viewed the world and how to contribute to it was cloaked in good, yet I wasn't aware of how my climb required an overhaul and alignment to the God of my faith. Therefore, my school leadership journey carved a peculiar pathway that would testify that "the toll of true leadership is heavy, and the more effective the leadership, the greater the cost" (J. O. Sanders 2007).

My Cross of Lack

"Lord, this can't be what you had in mind," my talk with God as I questioned my move to a school with limited funds, personnel, and resources. In this moment, my training as a tutor teacher, program coordinator, instructional specialist, assistant principal, and early years of leadership couldn't fathom why God would allow me to create a new school with the bare minimum. I remember going to Target and Walmart, purchasing my own office supplies, microwave, coffee maker and furniture. I questioned my entire move to another district, and even why I decided to stay in education. My husband's past comments of "Erica, you have the talent and skill to do well in corporate," echoed in my thoughts as I realized this new adventure. Tyrone, kept telling me multiple times, "Erica, your leadership would allow you to move in other industries, you don't have to stay in education." So, imagine my thoughts when I made the choice to leave school districts to open a school with minimal resources.

At this moment, I sought God. I knew that the success of what He was going to allow me to build was dependent on Him, yet I needed faith, therefore, the story of Gideon in the book of Judges became my lifeline. In Judges, the God of Abraham, Isaac, and Jacob called Gideon to judge the Israelites and conquer the Midianite army. Gideon questioned his ability and right to lead his nation. He couldn't believe that God would choose him for such an assignment as he was from the weakest clan in Manasseh and the youngest in his father's house. And like Gideon, I questioned my ability and worth, as well as scrutinized how my ethnicity, gender, intellectual and physical ability lead to swarming doubts in my head.

My first year of opening the school, I did not have a school secretary, assistant principal and other school support staff traditionally assigned to schools. Public education, while tasked with the assignment to educate and train students, is a deeply underfunded institution. The role of public schools currently applies an unforgiving pressure on educators to teach, train, counsel and support the needs of students and their families. Therefore, my question to God on how I was supposed to build a new school and lead the school community to success with limited funds and resources was a genuinely Gideon like response. In that position, I learned quickly how to move as an administrator, counselor, intervention specialist, test coordinator, data analyst, club sponsor, clerk etc. all in one. Encompassing multiple roles and duties became part of the cross that I wore. As I jumped from meeting to meeting, I developed a system of efficiently capturing new information, processing it quickly, organizing, and sharing it out as an action plan.

I remember attending a principal's meeting typing the presenter's notes on my laptop. Next to me was another principal who normally used his laptop during meetings. As the presenter's session closed out, I went to take a break when one of my superiors redirected me to put my laptop away so that I could pay attention to the meeting. My superior made this statement, "you are a leader." Very confused by this statement, I looked on as a deer in head lights, with a reply of "what/huh?" He replied, "you are a leader now, you should act like it" in reference to my laptop being open during the meeting. At this point I was confused by the statement as this was the first time, I had ever had a conversation with this superior. And for the initial communication to be an open rebuke in front of another one of my colleagues left a sour taste in my mouth. I was boiling inside, and I didn't say what I wanted to say. But what I wondered in that same vein was if he was going to correct my white male colleague regarding the same "inappropriate" behavior. I did not feel the need to tell him that I was typing notes from the meeting as I was flabbergasted at the entire situation. I walked away wondering if the intersectionality of who I was played a role in the rebuke as it is common for our society to question the professionalism and competence of others who have a difference in appearance. Was it my age, ethnicity, gender or misunderstanding of learning styles, I'm not sure. However, not rebuking my colleague for the same instance led me to accept ethnicity and gender as a factor. I don't know if I became more agitated by his misperception of my lack of leadership qualities or how this event further exacerbated disparities in education. When you become adjusted to working with a lack of resources and staff, you learn how to move efficiently and innovatively so that you can accomplish all the things. Because of our campus' small enrollment and staff, I did not have support staff to delegate administrative and planning items to. So during principal and administrator meetings, I developed a habit of quickly recording information from the meeting, processing it on the spot, and turning it into an action plan during the meeting because if I didn't type the notes in the meeting, when I went back to campus, I would be flooded with a barrage of others items to address without time to follow up with the directives given in our principal meetings. This one example of what it takes to move through lack became an ongoing thorn in my discussion with God. As a one-woman administration team, I learned different facets of school management and operation because I ended up needing to execute multiple tasks given. So my conversation with God went like this, "Now I don't know how I'm supposed to build a new school, ensure these students graduate with their high school diploma and associate degree, with limited staffing, time and funds in comparison to the surrounding schools around me. Are you sure you want me here? This can't be what you had planned for me."

Gideon had his moments as well, "please, my Lord. How can I save Israel? Indeed, my clan is the weakest in Manasseh, and I am the youngest in my father's house" (Judges 6:15 Berean). Just like Gideon, I asked God plenty of questions so that I could receive His instruction and wisdom throughout my years in the principalship. When God dwindled Gideon's army from 30,000 to 300, I felt seen. God told Gideon, "You have too many people for Me to deliver Midian into their hands, lest Israel glorify themselves over Me, saying, 'My own hand has saved me'" (Judges 7:2 Berean).

God's response to Gideon echoed to me as we served under 300 students with 16 staff members. And in the first two years of our new school, we had 4-6 full-time staff members that formed the foundation of our campus. As our school grew, God's hand covered and protected us with a constant reminder to me, that to move in success, I had to strip myself of pride, independence, and trust in the Holy One. And that my trusting of God meant that I had to trust Him even when it didn't make sense. As God delivered Midian and the whole camp into Gideon's sword, God allowed an extraordinary success for the school community. Our first graduating class had an 82% associate degree completion, followed by an increase to 89% for the following graduating class. The most current graduating class surpassed the first two classes with 100% associate degree attainment. And while I contributed our success to our staff, students, parents and intentional student support systems, if it had not been for our faith, we would not have a story to tell. Remember, what God told Gideon, that he had "too many people" (Judges 7:2 Berean). When we move with faith, submitted to God's authority, we cannot take credit for our victory, "lest Israel glorify themselves over Me, saying, "My own hand has saved me" (Judges 7:2 Berean).

This experience allowed me to put trust into the people God assigned to me by supporting them as they grew in their personal and professional walk. I quickly learned how to best serve my staff and provide them with optimum opportunities for them to learn, plan, execute and adjust their work. I adopted a way of innovating, taking risks and creating a safe space for teachers to do the same while focusing on instruction and student learning. This may have meant that I absorbed the burden of societal, community and district initiatives to protect the staff's time. With new and younger staff, I carved out weekly check-in meetings with them as needed so that I could get a pulse of their confidence, support their instructional goals, and train them on our school processes. Coordinating teachers with curriculum leaders, mentor teachers and outside learning opportunities became a norm. Studying the team, embracing their strengths, while recognizing weak areas was an all-consuming task of building school culture.

I remember when our school did get to hire a secretary, she would always ask, do you need anything? It was my focus to ensure that our teachers had the supplies, materials, and equipment that they needed. I also believe that I became comfortable with lack, that I didn't want others to share in my experiences. Therefore, creating incentives, constant communication, adjusting our processes, edifying our learning community became part of our system.

Developing as a leader included an abundance of prayer, bible study, biblical application, personal and professional development, late nights and ongoing communication and collaboration with my team, students, parents, and other educational leaders. I sacrificed a lot of time and energy away from my family to focus on building the community. In this journey, the consistent stripping of self, pride, independence, and my own strength seemed to be a reoccurring theme. You cannot move in your own strength as a leader. When the time came to hire more staff, prayer became my go to, as I needed to hire staff that could find success in a small learning community. When you work at a small school, you easily wear multiple hats due to the needs of the campus. Where our campus lacked, grace did abound.

My Cross of Adversity

My bottom-line as a collegiate school principal meant that our campus needed to graduate high school seniors with an associate degree. The burden of graduating college ready students would be our mission, and we would commit to developing instructional and social processes that would move us to our goal; therefore, the book of Nehemiah became an integral read for me especially in the face of adversity.

Since my adolescent years, I always felt a stirring to grow and edify others so that they too have an opportunity to accept and work the calling on their life. Nehemiah also had a stirring to rebuild not only the walls of Jerusalem, but the community (Nehemiah 1 Berean).

When King Artaxerxes granted Nehemiah leave from his cup bearing duties to restore the wall, he endured mockery and opposition from his local haters: Sanballat, Tobiah and Geshem. Sanballat ridiculed the Jews before the public by saying, "What are these feeble Jews doing? Can they restore the wall by themselves? Will they offer sacrifices? Will they complete it in a day? Can they bring these burnt stones back to life from the mounds of rubble" (Nehemiah 4: 2-3 Berean)?

And likewise, I recall the first few years of opening the campus hearing similar Sanballat like sentiments such as:

- "All of your students are going to fail out of the program."
- "There is no way you are going to be able to get these kids to graduate with an associate degree."
- "How are they going to pass college classes?"
- "Wait, are you the principal?"

- "You know, they don't really care about your program."
- "You are not doing enough."
- "Why are you using our resources?"

I could go on about the type of response and feedback received from educators, community members and parents alike, but I rather underscore the point that no one is immune to adversity, especially if you are called to lead. The spirit of Tobiah, Sanballat, Geshem is a universal spirit of mockery, deception and hate designed to distract you from your bottom-line or purpose. Therefore, like Nehemiah, transformative leaders must deepen their faith walk so we are not distracted by those sent to wreak havoc on our work. You cannot control someone who tries to forge a plan to confuse, frustrate and destroy the work, but you can control your response, which can impact your success.

In 2021 our campus had a school shooting, now if I haven't communicated this before, our campus was a split campus. We had 9th and 10th graders housed in a comprehensive high school and 11th and 12th graders located at our local community college. And that year, boy, was Tobiah and his friends stirring the pot of adversity. The shooting occurred on the comprehensive high school with our lower grades. That year we were also preparing to graduate our 2nd graduating class. With the ongoing public meetings, news coverage, mental health needs of staff and students, student's academic needs, readjusting safety and security protocol, merged with COV19 protocol, it seemed as if I fell into an abyss. Any idea of self-care and healing I may have needed, I buried it inside because I wanted to serve and ensure that everyone else was fine. I did not see a counselor or therapist, even though I recommended everyone else to do so. I rarely took days off, even though I implored my staff to take their days off. Pushing self-care for others, while neglecting mine, was the theme of that year. I redirected my thoughts towards supporting the mental and social needs of our 9th and 10th grade campus, while intensifying our academic support plan for our 11th and 12th graders. It was a year of limited sleep, late nights, early mornings, public meetings, and constant hustle. And even as I attempted to readjust our school plan, it never seemed to be enough. I remember getting emails from parents:

- Stop sending all these emails.
- Where have you been, I haven't heard from you all year?
- You have not done anything for my child. Ugh, I hate it here.
- You don't care about my child.
- Stop calling me.

And even as the pot stirrers kept delivering their messages, reflecting on Nehemiah's discipline to not get off the wall and focus on the work inspired me. I'm reminded of what Nehemiah proclaimed to his haters. He said, that the "God of heaven is the One who will grant us success. We, His servants, will start rebuilding..." (Nehemiah 2:20 Berean).

In the face of mockery, ridicule and lack, Nehemiah focused on repairing the walls of Jerusalem. When discouragement, divisiveness and accusative spirits grew, Nehemiah focused on rebuilding the wall. He zoned in on praying to God, galvanizing his team, supporting his team, communicating, and recommunicating the mission, making necessary adjustments (building the wall with a weapon in hand), avoiding distractions so that the community could rebuild and secure the wall together. In the end, Nehemiah, led the rebuilding of the wall, initiated worship and reverence to God, established order and processes, sought the necessary resources for the community and closed out his assignment with the final plea to God, "Remember me, O my God, with favor" (Nehemiah 13:31 Berean). What an amazing, yet humble mic drop moment for Nehemiah.

At the end of that school year, our graduating class had an 89% associate degree completion rate. And while certain sentiments rung in our ear such as, "the school still not do enough," Nehemiah's prayer and God's grace rings louder.

What is your cross?

There is no way we can avoid adversity and the sense of lack in our leadership journey. Carrying our cross requires a stripping of self so that we can allow God's grace to work to, in and through us. Just as Nehemiah had to endure adversity and how Gideon overcame deficit thinking, what areas of growth are you being called to address? What have you been called to do? What is your cross? While your journey requires a stripping of self, our letting go would never compare to the stripping that Jesus Christ endured for all of humanity. Jesus Christ, a perfect model of leadership, is calling us all to our purpose. Will you pick up your cross?

Leadership Meditation

In the principalship, I reflected on a few scriptures about humility, personal accountability, trust, work, identity, and wisdom. When I fought against my own pride, I prayed scriptures that endowed me with humility. When I needed reminders about the weight of leadership, I prayed scriptures that helped with my personal accountability. During moments when I needed to rely on God, proclaiming scriptures of trust strengthen me. In those dark moments of wanting to throw in the towel, I had to reflect on the "why" of the work. For the times when I sought instruction, I looked to what the Word of God said about wisdom.

The following scriptures will anchor your soul throughout your leadership journey. This is not an exhaustive list of scripture references. I pray that you will meditate on these scriptures as you move in your God ordained calling. May you find wisdom, peace, and victory as you move in your season.

Humility

Lord, thou hast heard the desire of the humble: thou wilt prepare their heart, thou wilt cause thine ear to hear.
Psalm 10:17

Better it is to be of an humble spirit with the lowly, than to divide the spoil with the proud.   Proverbs 16:19

He hath shown thee, O man, what is good: and what doth the Lord require of thee, but to do justly, and to love mercy, and to walk humbly with thy God?
Micah 6:8

But he giveth more grace. Wherefore he saith, God resisteth the proud, but giveth grace unto the humble.   James 4:6

Trust

Offer the sacrifices of righteousness and put your trust in the Lord.

Psalm 4:5

And they that know thy name will put their trust in thee: For thou, Lord has not forsaken them that seek thee.
Psalm 9:10

Trust in him at all times; ye people, pour out your heart before him: God is a refuge for us. Psalm 62:8

Trust in the LORD with all thine heart; and lean not unto thine own understanding. In all thy ways acknowledge him, and he shall direct thy paths.
Proverbs 3:5-6

Accountability

This book of the law shall not depart out of thy mouth; but thou shalt meditate therein day and night, that thou mayest observe to do according to all that is written therein: for then thou shalt make thy way prosperous, and then thou shalt have good success.
Joshua 1:8

And if thou wilt walk before me, as David thy father walked, in integrity of heart, and in uprightness, to do according to all that I have commanded thee, and wilt keep my statutes and my judgments.
1 Kings 9:4

For if thou altogether holdest thy peace at this time, then shall their enlargement and deliverance arise to the Jews from another place; but thou and thy father's house shall be destroyed: and who knoweth whether thou art come to the kingdom for such a time as this? Esther 4:14

My brethren, be not many masters, knowing that we shall receive the greater condemnation. James 3:1

That the trial of your faith, being much more precious than of gold that perisheth, though it be tried with fire, might be found unto praise and honour and glory at the appearing of Jesus Christ. 1 Peter 1:7

Identity

And be not conformed to this world: but be ye transformed by the renewing of your mind, that ye may prove what *is* that good, and acceptable, and perfect, will of God.
Romans 12:2

Therefore, if any man be in Christ, he is a new creature: old things are passed away; behold, all things are become new.
2 Corinthians 5:17

I am crucified with Christ: nevertheless, I live; yet not I, but Christ liveth in me: and the life which I now live in the flesh I live by the

faith of the Son of God, who loved me, and gave himself for me.
Galatians 2:20

But ye are a chosen generation, a royal priesthood, an holy nation, a peculiar people; that ye should shew forth the praises of him who hath called you out of darkness into his marvelous light.
1 Peter 2:9

Wisdom

And Gideon said unto God, Let not thine anger be hot against me, and I will speak but this once: let me prove, I pray thee, but this once with the fleece; let it now be dry only upon the fleece, and upon all the ground let there be dew.
Judges 6:39

The LORD taketh my part with them that help me: therefore shall I see my desire upon them that hate me. It is better to trust in the LORD than to put confidence in man.
Psalm 118:7-8

And the spirit of the LORD shall rest upon him, the spirit of wisdom and understanding, the spirit of counsel and might, the spirit of knowledge and of the fear of the LORD; And shall make him of quick understanding in the fear of the LORD: and he shall not judge after the sight of his eyes, neither reprove after the hearing of his ears.

Isaiah 11:2-4

If any of you lack wisdom, let him ask of God, that giveth to all men liberally, and upbraideth not; and it shall be given him.

James 1:5

Work

Whatsoever thy hand findeth to do, do *it* with thy might; for there *is* no work, nor device, nor knowledge, nor wisdom, in the grave, whither thou goest.

Ecclesiastes 9:10

And let the beauty of the LORD our God be upon us: and establish thou the work of our hands upon us; yea, the work of our hands establish thou it.

Psalm 90:17

Let your light so shine before men, that they may see your good works, and glorify your Father which is in heaven.

Matthew 5:16

I have glorified thee on the earth: I have finished the work which thou gavest me to do. John 17:4

Principal Bennett, thank you for participating in my first anthology. As a principal, wife, and mother I know your days are full, so to take the time out of your busy schedule to do this makes my heart glad. Thank you for sharing your journey of leadership with us and I pray this is just the beginning of a new chapter in your life. May God bless you and keep you.

Dr. Yvonne Henderson

Failure Is Not Final

By Dr. Yvonne Henderson

How many times have you started something and because it failed, you thought it was over? I have found myself in that situation so many times, especially when it comes to love. You would think love is easy to find when you know how to love, or at least you think you do.

Like most people I am sure you have been in more than one relationship over the course of your lifespan. If you have been in more than one, that means you have had some relationships that have failed. It may not have been because of you, and it may have. You may not look at it as a failure, but if it did not work for whatever reason, it failed. What happened? It could be several things that cause a relationship to fail. Over the years I have had several failed relationships. You look back over your life and try to figure out where did everything go wrong. Why is it that my relationships don't work.

The first relationship, or sign of love we ever encounter is from childhood. How your parents show love and interact is very important to how your relationship structure will develop. I thought my parents had the perfect relationship until I got old enough to understand. My dad would drink and become very abusive verbally to my mom. Then would argue and at one point I thought that was normal. Until it became physical. I vowed never to let a man put his hands on me. My first encounter with love was in high school. I met a guy and we hit it off. I was a virgin and wasn't thinking about having sex. I thought he really liked me. He asked me to our Senior Prom, I was excited. I went shopping and bought a dress, heels and got make-up. Know you may not think much of that, but I was a Tomboy, and a dress was not something you ever find me in. So, for me to get a dress for the occasion and the guy it had to be serious. Well, there I was in my light blue chiffon dress waiting to be picked up. One hour, two hours, three hours passed, and he never showed up or called. When I got to school that Monday, he wasn't there, I thought maybe something had happened. Tuesday he was there, and he avoided me like I had done something wrong. He wouldn't talk to me. People were pointing and making fun of me. I felt so low and didn't even know why because I had done nothing but wait for him and he stood me up. I was really hurt; it took me a long time to get over that. Failure number one.

I tried love yet again after high school, I met this gentleman at church. He was a college student and I thought that was cool, but that excitement soon came to a screeching halt when I found out he had a girlfriend at college. Still a virgin I was being pressured to have sex. I wasn't ready and did not want to. He told me if I loved him, I would do it. I thought he was the once, so I tried it, I couldn't go through with it because it hurt, and I made him stop. Needless to say, the relationship was over after that I was confused because I felt, if you are in the church, we sing in the choir together, how are you asking me to do this? You know that is not right. He went back to school and sent me a long letter telling me it was over because his girlfriend at school was willing to give it up. Failure number two.

Met another young man in church, he was a minister I was trying so hard not to find someone like my dad that I was literally running into the arms of men who were just like him, or at least reminded me of him. This one was also in the military, I guess you could say I was stricken by the uniform. I loved a man in uniform. We courted for a while and things seemed to be going great. He proposed and I said yes, we went and looked at the rings. I should have known something was not right when he asked me to co-sign the loan for the rings. After a month he was discharged from the military, I didn't find out until much later that it was a dishonorable discharge, which meant he did not get any military benefits. Well, I didn't think that was going to be a problem because he would get a job. Well, come to find out there was something mentally wrong as to why he was discharged. I began to think, "this is nothing like my dad." He packed and moved back to his hometown of College Park, GA. He asked me to go, but we weren't married yet and I told him I would wait until after the wedding, since we would be getting married on February 14th, that all came to a halt when he had a stroke in December of the preceding year. You would think I would remember the year this all happened, but it alludes me at this time. After he was home from the hospital his mom called me to tell me what was going on. I told her I would fly out on February 13th to be by his side since we were supposed to spend the rest of our lives together. When I arrived in GA, he was very standoffish and nasty towards me. I could not figure out why. Then I noticed a young lady there taking care of him and he informed me that she had been there for him the whole time and he was in love with her and did not want me. His mom told him he was wrong for doing me that way, but he did not care. I asked her to take me back to the hotel and I would leave in the morning. She offered for me to stay with them so I wouldn't have to spend that money since she said we were almost family. She was not happy with what her son had done. Failed relationship number three.

    I probably didn't mention it, but my father was a ex-military, a police officer, and later in life became a minister of the Gospel. I am praying at this point for God to do something different. Will I ever find true love? I thought about just giving up on love, men, relationships and the whole nine, but I wasn't even 21 yet. I still had a lot of life to live and more things to experience. Boy did I have more to experience.

He found me, after the last failed relationship, I decided to go visit my sister in Chicago and I went to church with her. This happened a couple of times and she called me and said, "the drummer wanted to know if he could have your number." I was taken back and a little excited that someone had noticed me and wanted to talk to me. So, I told her she could give him my number. He called, we conversed, and I grew to like him. I was a little leery because he was a minister. He asked me to come to Chicago to see him. I didn't think there would be any harm in that, so I went. It was nice, we went to dinner at Fuddruckers, I look back on it know and think, "what a cheap date." I had not been on very many dates and was happy to have someone show a little interest. That's when things began to spiral down. My self-worth was being compromised. When I visited it would stay with my sister and he would pick me up. As we got closer, I began to stay at his place. Life was looking up, so I thought. The first couple of times I stayed with him it was nice nothing happened, but it happened, he wanted to have sex, I was still a virgin I was 22 years old and had never been with a man and he was 10 years older than me. This was more pressure; would I be able to tell him no and he be okay with it? Well, the first couple of times it worked, but things got heated. He was the first man to perform oral sex on me and I believe I lost my mind. He did this before we ever had intercourse, then one day we tried it and it hurt like all get out. I could not understand what all the fuss was about, because I really didn't like it. The one thing that I feared was being rejected after giving myself to someone, and that is exactly what happened. After we had intercourse, he stopped calling, texting, or responding to me. When we finally communicated, he apologized and informed me he had been doing a lot of preaching, because he was looking to have his own church and wanted to know if I was ready to be a First Lady. I went running back excited for him and I thought it would be great. Time went on and he got the call to pastor, he was going to be installed and I thought, "Wow! I'm going to be a First Lady." Well, that didn't happen. I came down for the weekend and stayed with him, helping him prepare for his big day, but the unthinkable happened, he said he did not want me to go to church with him, but to meet him there. I was confused. I got there, I sat in the back of the church, once the service was over, he came to me, hugged me and introduced me to his mother as a friend. We went downstairs for dinner after church, but I was not invited to sit with him, I was at some random table. I called my cousin and asked her to pick me up. I left and went home with her. After everything was over, I met up with him, got my things from his apartment and went home. Once back home, I asked, "What was that all about? He said he realized that

I would not be First Lady material and did not want to give me the wrong impression. Needless to say, this was the end of that relationship. Failure number four.

This was the last straw I was determined not to ever get into another relationship. A year of chaos ensued, I began to party and stay out late. I didn't think God was really going to do what He said. I had saved myself and wanted to be married, the one man I trusted with not only my heart, but my body rejected me after he got what he wanted and then said I was unworthy to be in his world. The biggest disappointment was he was a man of God and was to live a certain way and I felt tainted and violated. From that point I had little respect for men especially those who called themselves men of God. I created my own path, doing what I wanted with whomever I wanted and not feeling any type of way about it. I didn't think I was worthy enough to be in a relationship.

I went off to college at age 24 and became even wilder by the age 26 I was working on my bachelor's, and I saw the man of my dreams; light skinned, tall, nice looking, oh my Gosh I felt like I had just seen an angel. I saw this man and the words that came out of my mouth was, "I'm going to marry him." One thing, I didn't even know his name, but I saw the uniform, he was one of the security guards on my campus. A few days went by before I saw him again, when I did, I made sure we talked. We made a connection; we were both from Illinois. He didn't realize I was from Illinois until he saw my car plates. I remember driving and him pulling me over in his police car, just to be able to talk to me. I thought that was sexy. I had said I would never get married and if I wasn't married by the time I was 30, I would adopt a child and be happy.

He was the one that made me change my ways and settle down to be with one person. After two years he came all the way to Illinois during Christmas break to ask my dad for my hand in marriage. I just knew he was a keeper. We got married on July 4th, because he said he wanted to go out of singlehood with a bang. It was a nice intimate ceremony with family and friends. I was 29, so I got what I asked for. Afterwards we moved back to Illinois so he could be near his family and my family. There were some good times and some bad times, but I guess you could say the good times outweighed the bad. I wanted to have a child, but I was told I could not have kids, or at least it would be very difficult for me to conceive. I was devastated because I wanted nothing more than to be a mom. I engulfed myself in getting my education and pursuing my career as an educator, so I enrolled in classes to complete my degrees, and subbed in surrounding districts to have some type of income. It seemed like the more time I spent at school the more distance was put into our marriage. You would have thought me furthering my education to better myself would be a good thing, but he didn't want me to do anything but stay in the house and cater to him. At least that's what I told myself, even though that wasn't what I was feeling. You may ask, "How do you know? Well, a woman can tell when things are going wrong in their Spirit. Things began to get worse; he would spend more and more time away from home, he would take his kids to another woman's house because he said I wasn't worthy to watch his kids. I wasn't stupid, but everything was confirmed when she had the audacity to call my house looking for him at 2:00 a.m. I knew there were things I would not tolerate, and this was one of them. I told him I wanted a divorce, and we would go our separate ways once I finished school. I was hurt, but we made a pact that, if one of us cheated we would cut our losses and go our separate ways. Since we did not have kids together, it would be easy to move on without any ties. Well, that idea came to a screeching holt when I found out I was four weeks pregnant. I tried to get a divorce, but in the state, we were in you could not get a divorce if you were pregnant for paternity reasons. Believe it or not, he had the nerve to doubt he was the father. I knew better. We separated, until after my son was born, we got back together, but he never stopped cheating. At my son's first birthday party, I told him I was done, and I was moving out. He told me I would never be able to make it on my own, but I had been saving to prepare for this, because I was not going to be treated this way. I moved out, not wanting to rent I investigated purchasing a house. Again, he told me I would never be able to do it without him. I prayed and asked God to move, so I would not be under his thumb the rest of my life. I found a house, but I was told I had to file for divorce otherwise his name would be on the house, so I filed. My divorce was final on October 21, and I closed on my house December 1. God was beginning to turn my life around, even though this was failed relationship number five.

I was looking at life in a whole different light now, I had a child to raise, it wasn't just me. The divorce was amicable, and we had joint custody, but I allowed my son to stay with his father, because I thought it would be the best thing for him. It hurt my heart every time I left him because he cried like I was leaving him with a total stranger. During this time, I did not date, because I did not want to bring anyone around my son if it wasn't serious. I had a few relationships here and there, but I never brought them to my house. Once I brought someone around my son and he had a whole fit, because he didn't want any other man around his mommy, except his dad, and sometimes he didn't want him to touch me.

Well that all ended when his father passed away. My son was ten and I turned into a beast. I did everything on my own because I figured all my relationships had failed, but I had something to hold on to from this last one. I raised my son the best I could as a woman and vowed to keep him safe, because if anything were to happen to him because of a man I was dating I would go to jail, and he would be a ward of the state. You see being molested at a young age by a relative made me leery about having my son around anyone other than myself. It was he and I against the world. He used to tease me about dating. I told him he could date when I started dating. There was one guy that he liked, and I thought it was going to work. He had a son and he had lost his mom. I had a son who had lost his dad. I thought it would be a perfect match. We That didn't last long, because the son that I would choose him over my own son, that would never happen and the dad thought he was just going to live off me and do nothing. His motives were all wrong and I could see it. Failed relationship number six.

After so many failed relationships I just had to begin to pray and trust God, I am getting too old to be chasing men, and that was the problem, I was chasing, but no one was chasing me. I came to the realization that I had to do something different to get a different result. I was tired of the same ole' type of guys, the ones who were intimidated by my strength, the young men who thought they had a sugar momma, and the older guys who just wanted me to sit back and retire, the ones that just wanted to hit it and not make a commitment. I was tired of hook ups and relationships that had no substance. I had to find my worth. I was worth more than that.

So, I had a conversation with God, or should I say,

"A Prayer For my Husband."

I asked Him to remove anything from me that was not lined up with His purpose for my life. Send me a man that would love me the way You the church. Send me a man that love You more than he loves me. Send me a man that will accept me the way I am, and accept my son, but not necessarily try to be a father to him since he is grown now, but can be a mentor, someone he can look up to and respect for loving and taking care of his mom. Send me a man who will love my Kittie as much as I do, that may sound strange to most, but my cat has been in my life for 17 years and she is not going anywhere. Father send me a man that will compliment me in ministry and understand what You have called me to do. Father, I just want someone to love, and someone to love me back, and Father send me someone who is close that I don't have to travel long distance to. Someone who is willing to come see me and not just me going to see them.

When I tell you God answers prayer and He answers quickly, not a month had gone by and the three guys that I had been talking to disappeared. I was hearing God, and I was out doing my thing minding my own business, when I met this amazing man

(Curtis) while a vender at The Sugar Rush *(The Sugar Shack as he calls it)*. It started as a business meeting to publish his story. Before we ended, he was praying for me and my son, I had never had a man pray for me and mine and sincerely mean it. Our first call was three hours, it went well beyond the scheduled consultation. From there we began spending more and more time on the phone. He gave me tips on how to handle my grown son. He said things would turn around quicker than I expected and low and behold they did. My son and I began working on our relationship. I was beginning to understand him, and it was a beautiful thing. I owed it all the Curtis who was and is very loving, caring and family oriented. He understood me, he got me. He was everything I had wanted and more, the only thing he was married, and I was not going to cross that line again. As time went on, we talked about that and he was waiting on an answer from God about what was going on with his marriage, we prayed together and waited on God. Through it all God has kept us. The divorce is final, and we are ready to embark on a new life together. I have never been happier in my entire life, at 58 God has blessed me with the Kingdom husband that I so deserve, after so many failed relationships, I believe I have learned how to make sure this one is final. Thank You God for the failed relationships that set me up and help prepare me for my final relationship. Failure is not final.

www.ingramcontent.com/pod-product-compliance
Lightning Source LLC
Chambersburg PA
CBHW072123070526
44585CB00016B/1535

*9 781734 420883 *